Lilian Mun...

I

MESSAGES FROM YOUR HEART

Beautiful ~ A Journal

Jacquelyn B. Fletcher

GOLD HOUSE PRESS
Books and gifts to evolve the human spirit

 Published 2014
Printed in the United States of America

Book and cover design by Cheryl Viker
Editing by Rebecca Rowell
Art photography by Patti Neil
Author photo by Joanna Proesser
Published by Gold House Press
P.O. Box 40, Lakeville, MN 55044
goldhousepress.com

To order in bulk or for wholesale pricing, contact the publisher at info@goldhousepress.com.

ISBN 978-1-941933-01-5 (softcover)

Dear You,

This is your place to write the messages your heart wants you to hear. All you need to do is close your eyes, tell your heart you're ready to listen, and see what comes. Your heart is wise. It's ready to open up to you. It wants to show you how beautiful you and your world are. You can do this. Be brave.

Love,

Jacque

OPEN

• Taking ~~[illegible]~~ challenging class & passing

- My Parent bringing me here
- Kitchen being decent
-

- Peace
- Friendly
- Confidence

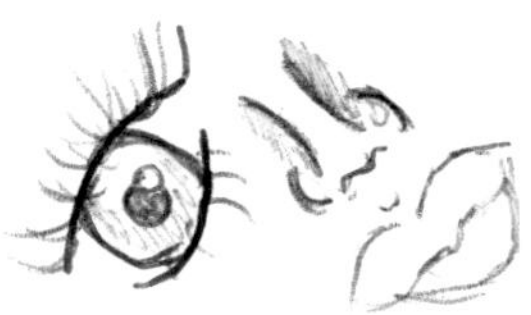

Sept 25 <u>Bible Study</u>

Ecclesiates 8:8 - No man has authority over the wind, to keep the wind; or is ruler over the day of death. In war no man's time is free, and evil will not keep sinner safe.

Ecclesiates 8:7 - we don't have much control of the future or death

Prayer + Faith = God answers

<u>Luke 13:6</u>

Love covers multitudes of sin

John 15:1-5

Psalm 128:1-3! Amen

God & Jesus bringing meaning to your life.

Lord I give you my heart
I give my soul → I LIVE 4 U
alone

Wednesday Service

Matthew 9:9 (HCSB)

Matthew 16:24 (KJV) 20-24

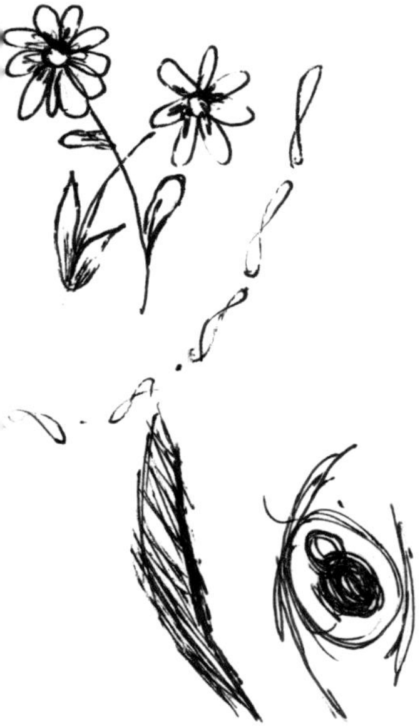

Hebrew 10:20

Isaiah 6:10

Luke 5:15

1 Thessalonians 5:27

Malachi 3:8!

YES

BRAVE

TRUE

HOPE

LOVE

About the Author

Jacquelyn B. Fletcher is an award-winning author and speaker. She's co-creator and host of the Healing Words television show and a founding faculty member of the Creative Writing at the Bedside program, both administered by the Mayo Clinic Dolores Jean Lavins Center for Humanities in Medicine in Rochester, Minnesota. Really, she's a transformation expert. She's lost 100 pounds and kept it off for nearly 20 years. Dug herself out of debt. And recovered from a broken heart again and again.

Her books and projects all aim to support healing, encourage empowerment, and inspire transformation.

To check out the collection of Dear You art and gifts, or to find out about having Jacquelyn speak to your group, visit **JacquelynFletcher.com**.

CPSIA information can be obtained at www.ICGtesting.com
Printed in the USA
BVOW11s0842011014

368982BV00009B/16/P

9 781941 933015